NEW! IMPROVED

BONUS FOR PROMPTNESS! Mail drawing in next 5 days—we'll send you valuable folder on How to Start In Commercial Art—FREE! *(PLEASE PRINT)*

The Greatest Girdle Buy in America!

TAKE MY ADVICE!

Loads of Fun and Useful, Too

LOVE CAN BE YOURS AGAIN!

The ads in *Hey Skinny!* have appeared in the following magazines: *Alarming Tales, Barnyard Comics, Blue Bolt, Boy Stories, The Brain, Buck Duck, Buzzy, Candy, Captain Marvel, Chief Wahoo, Coo Coo, Crime & Justice, Crime and Punishment, Dagwood, Dodo the Frog, Famous Funnies, Feature Comics, Frankenstein, Fritzi Ritz, Funny Animals, Future World, Gabby, Giggle, Hap Hazard, Heart Throbs, Inky & Dinky, Komik Pages, Krazy Komics, Leading Comics, Little Bit, Little Eva, Little Lulu, Love Confessions, Love Letters, Love Secrets, Lucky Duck, Marmaduke Mouse, Marvin Mouse, Mickey Finn, Mighty Mouse, Muggy-Doo Boy Cat, Mutt & Jeff, My Friend Irma, Nancy & Sluggo, Nellie the Nurse, Patsy & Her Pals, Peter Cottontail, Punch & Judy, George Pal's Puppetoons, Ribtickler, Romeo Tubbs, Sad Sack, Scream Comics, Silly Toons, Sparkle, Sparkling Stars, Super Rabbit, Terry and the Pirates,* and *Tip Top.*

Printed in the United States of America.
Library of Congress Cataloging-in-Publication Data:
Hey Skinny!: great advertisements from the Golden Age of comics books/ [compiled by] Miles Beller and Jerry Leibowitz. p. cm.
ISBN 0-8118-0828-9
1. Comic books, strips, etc.— History and criticism. 2. Comic books, strips, etc., in advertising. 3. Advertising— Comic art paraphernalia. I. Beller, Miles. II. Leibowitz, Jerry. III. Title: Great advertisements from the Golden Age of comic books.
PN6710.H48 1995
741.6'7'09–dc20   94-21428 CIP

Book and cover design: Douglas P. Becker

Distributed in Canada by Raincoast Books
8680 Cambie Street, Vancouver, B.C. V6P 6M9

10 9 8 7 6 5 4 3 2 1

Chronicle Books
275 Fifth Street
San Francisco, CA 94103

For Eli Charles Beller, who laughs long and often.

For my parents,
Erwin and Julie Leibowitz,
who had the good sense to start me reading
comic books at an early age.

The authors would like to thank photographer
Jim Reisman for his sharp, knowing eye.

Hey SKINNY!

Great Advertisements from the Golden Age of Comic Books

MILES BELLER &
JERRY LEIBOWITZ
PREFACE BY JAY CHIAT

CHRONICLE BOOKS
SAN FRANCISCO

RECKMOBI
GOLLY! IT HIT
HE WALL SO FAST
T BROKE!
DIDN'T! SEE? IT ALL FITS
OGETHER IN A JIFFY!
, YOU TRY IT!
$2.98
NEW AND DIFFER

I began looking at comic books at the newsstand on the corner of Holland and Lydig Avenues in The Bronx. I would sit on a stack of newspapers, devouring as many comics as I could before I was told to stop mutilating the magazines and either buy or shove off.

That's probably where I developed my high anxiety, trying to get through all the new arrivals before I was thrown out. If I were successful, I'd be able to spend the dime my mother had given me on junk candy instead of a comic book. My favorite candies were those little colored sugar dots glued to paper, followed closely by chocolate licorice. Chocolate licorice . . . the first oxymoron.

Although Superman was hot even then, Batman and Robin were my favorites. When I was seven my Aunt Frances made me a Robin costume for a neighborhood Halloween party held in the basement of our apartment house. Although my hopes were high, none of the girls made a fuss over me. This, probably my first bout with female rejection, led to mild depression.

It was the forties, and girlie magazines hadn't been invented yet—even if they had, they weren't readily available to a seven year old. So my sexual awakening was kindled by Sheena, Queen of the Jungle, the heroine of Jumbo comics. This scantily-clad temptress with the impressive cleavage was much more provocative to me than the topless natives in National Geographic.

DRAW ME!

r A Free $280 Art Course!

mplete $280 Art Courses, including Drawing Outfits!

try for a prize! Find out if you have profitable
nothing to lose—everything to gain. Mai

ents not eligible. Make
lettering. All dra
Winners not

HINGED LID

YOUR NAME

Only $1⁹⁸
Your Name
Engraved in
23 Karat Gold
without
Extra Cost

But just as enticing as the comic books' fantasy-filled stories were its stimulating ads. Who could resist a necktie that glowed in the dark and guaranteed a kiss? I remember that in high school the phrase "Will you kiss me in the dark, baby?" was as much a part of teenage jargon as "Get a life" is today. I remember this as a time when all of the boys' wallets had a condom imprint, though none of us actually had the opportunity to use one.

The one product I finally sent for was the amazing Vacutex, which was so powerful that it actually sucked blackheads right out of your face. Of course, blackhead squeezing and pimple popping were daily rituals during those oily puberty years. Yet beauty had its price. After my first Vacutex treatment I didn't go out in public for two days.

My only regret is that I never sent for the book *How to Write Love Letters*. Maybe if I had, those girls at the Halloween party would have noticed me in my Robin costume.

Jay Chiat

**if** as Zelda Fitzgerald wrote, we grow up "founding our dreams on the infinite promise of American advertising," the comic book ad has truly shaped our appetites and desires.

Long before art movements such as Pop appropriated the image of a muscle-bound bully kicking sand at a terrified wimp, before post-modern philosophers canonized the image of a ravaged dishpan hand, the cheap advertisements crammed into comic books of the 1940s and 1950s were an essential part of the American experience, revealing more about the national character than the tony appeals in more respectable publications.

Considering that some six to seven billion comic books were produced from 1940 to 1960, and that more comic books have been printed and bought than all the top-ten best-selling books of the last half century, the impact of comic book advertisements cannot be underestimated. By the early 1940s, 15 million comic books were published monthly in the United States, and during the 1950s the number soared to nearly 75 million, with an average of 15 comic books read each month by every other household in America. And tucked inside each comic book were numerous ads.

Yet numbers and statistics, however impressive, cannot illuminate why a form of "low" mass advertising—which first emerged as a modern form of advertising in 1935's *New Fun* comics—has so thoroughly captivated generations of Americans. One must revisit the 1940s and '50s, when, after a hesitant start in the '30s,

in-your-face advertising inundated the comics, brandishing lurid colors and brazenly peddling miraculous transformation. One could buy a toy pistol that "cracks out like a real gun" and a "life-like" rubber skull, "hideously real." It was a time when nothing was impossible—that is, if the ad hit the right hyperbolic pitch.

In the 1940s, while Frank Sinatra buckled bobby-soxers' knees, comic book ads helped readers "Make Your Own Records" for $8.49 plus postage. And as the unfriendly atom threatened to fracture the future, a comics ad announced a "new sensational offer to readers" wherein they could procure a "war surplus" gas mask, "released by the U.S. government." Comics were thick with all manner of superhero and -heroine—The Flame, Miss Fury, The Fighting Yank, Bullet Man, Captain Marvel (who outsold Superman), Wonder Woman, Captain America, Black Condor, Green Lantern—

supreme do-righters and buffed patriots accomplishing feats far beyond garden-variety mortals. Even that modern man-made substance plastic gave rise to an elastic mensch, Plastic Man ("Plas" to in-the-know fans), "His only weapon being his ability to bend, twist, or mold into any shape!!" Comic book readers looking to profit from this malleable material could send off for the Plastikit, with which they could "make $100 worth of valuable plastic objects for only $1.98 plus postage."

In addition to fantastic titans, average all-Americans such as redheaded Archie Andrews and his high school cohorts, who harkened back to everyteens Henry Aldrich and Andy Hardy from the '30s, found favor with readers. While in the late '40s strapless bras, lamp-shade hats, shoulder bags, and Dior's "New Look" were fashion's latest thing, the comic books advertised Twin Allure stick cologne and stick deodorant, which promised to help women get that man "and hold him!" Comic book readers followed the exploits of caped, cowled, and masked champions, and sent away for such must-haves as glow-in-the-dark "Kiss Me" neckties ("Girls can't resist") or primers on "How to get into the movies," which were guaranteed to improve the earthly plight of those lacking bullet-proof physiques or infinitely extrudable body parts.

As the '40s gave way to the '50s, Ike puttered on the golf course and Americans retreated to a new paradise, the suburbs. Ginsberg and the Beats howled estrangement, Little Richard wailed "tutti frutti," Elvis moaned "be-bop-a-loo-bop," "juvenile delinquents" became big-screen rebels, and *Blondie Comics Monthly*

offered a free copy of "Dagwood Splits the Atom" ("Authentic! Exciting! Amazing!"). Flipping through comics of the day, one encountered stories of loss and redemption, despair and renewal, or heartbreakers of a different order—Richie Rich and Dennis the Menace. Film and comics burst with 3-D, Superman, Batman, and Mighty Mouse leaping off the newsprint. Sci-fi, supernatural, and futuristic space oddities became comic books' everyday ethos, as in EC's *Weird Tales*. Living-room Philcos broadcast *I Love Lucy* and *I Married Joan,* versions of American life more daydream than fact; Jackson Pollock flung house paint onto yards of canvas; Senator Joe McCarthy improvised lists of cutthroat Commies; and Grace Kelly quit America to marry nobility in Monaco. But for those non-royals still searching for that "Dancing, Prancing Kind of Footwear," Thom McAnn peddled its "Hoe-Down" shoe in the comic book—at $7.95, a bargain.

In the mid-'50s, a New York psychiatrist named Dr. Frederick Wertham, author of *Seduction of the Innocent,* damned cultural offshoots such as comics as corrupters of youth. At the same time, a series of Congressional hearings on the graphic depiction of violence and sex in the pulps captured headlines and put the heat on comic book publishers. So chastened, they hastily set up their own restrictive rules under an entity called the Comics Code Authority. The CCA implemented a set of commandments forbidding such scandalous offenses as ". . . horror, excessive bloodshed, gory or gruesome crimes, depravity, lust, sadism, and masochism."

But the garish comic book ads would not die. And so late into the 1950s they continued, affirming the curative power of consumerism by promoting new and improved states of human happiness attainable only through acquisition. Contentment lay enticingly within one's grasp. Who could possibly resist such absurdly tantalizing items as a "racing turtle" with your name painted on its back ("All Turtles Guaranteed Alive on Delivery"), or a 10-day home trial of the Vacutex pimple remover ("Ugly Blackheads out in Seconds with Vacutex!")? With their pulsating saffron coupons, scarlet-bordered giveaways, and jet-black, cut-along-the-dotted-line solicitations, ads spoke of lives inalterably changed ("I am so thrilled as to how beautiful and white my teeth are from using WYTEN"), assuring satisfaction eternal ("Or your money back. Guaranteed!").

Unrepentant and unbowed, comic book advertisements stand as a scrappy, low-culture rebuff to the "science" of Madison Avenue, as shameless pleas to buy, and buy, and buy. Eschewing polished campaign strategies and big-budget financing, the pulp pitches pounced on the libido with gleeful ferocity.

In comic books' grainy formative days, only small, spirited firms with more moxie than money would venture into the untamed medium. But when the mix of visual hyperbole and written overstatement successfully coalesced, legions of youngsters and more than a few adults impetuously mailed off for that top-secret spy decoder ring or full-length, non-flammable wig.

Why do nervy ads from yellowed comics still act on us? In informal interviews, several experts gave their opinions. Maggie Thompson, co-editor of *Comic Buyer's Guide* and *Comic Buyer's Guide Price Guide* thinks these printed plugs demand strong participation and involvement. "While TV is passive, its commercials just coming out at you, reading the ads in comics is active." Tom Ballou, vice president of advertising for DC Comics, attributes the ads' persistence to their particular readers. "Whereas readers of magazines tend to skim the articles, the comic book reader pays close attention to everything, including the ads." Comics readers also keep their books for collections. Comics ads let readers "buy into" the illusion of mystery and magic that is the comic book's province.

Paul Curtis, fan club manager and archivist for Marvel Comics, suggests that the lasting influence and persistence of the comic book ad is underscored by a range of original work derived from them. A song in the movie *The Rocky Horror Picture Show* concerns body-building ads; a faux ad in *National Lampoon* urges readers to send for pet Sea Poodles; and *Mad* magazine paid early satirical tribute to the comic book advertisement by running a mail-order spoof of the genre on its March 1955 cover. Even contemporary comic books, Curtis says, cannot escape the early ads' immense gravitational pull: an ongoing story in *Doom Patrol* features a character who becomes the beefcake of the old muscle-man promotions.

The "golden age" of comic book advertising ended at the dawn of the psychedelic, TV-saturated 1960s, when mind-bending reality became stranger than even the quirkiest comic book appeals. Today, however, comic book ads of yesteryear occupy a venerated position in contemporary art circles. Once condemned as insidious cons, they are now celebrated as cherished icons.

In *Hey Skinny!* we have gathered the most memorable and incendiary ads. These ads appeared in many different comics at many different times. The dates under these ads refer to the editions from which the image was photographed. Brash, bold, and uncompromising, they are graphically compelling and textually captivating. Having read through thousands of comics, we chose those ads that stand as shining examples of naked hyperbole and unfettered hype.

Today, long after the professional bluenoses and sanctimonious moralizers have been hushed, the comic book advertisements of the '40s and '50s continue on their idiosyncratic way. Emblems of the collective culture, enshrined like sacred tableaus depicting consumerism's oddball saints, these irrepressible graphic artifacts disregard conventional logic. They continue to entertain, enrich, and enliven the American scene in matters high, low, and in-between.

Miles Beller
Jerry Leibowitz

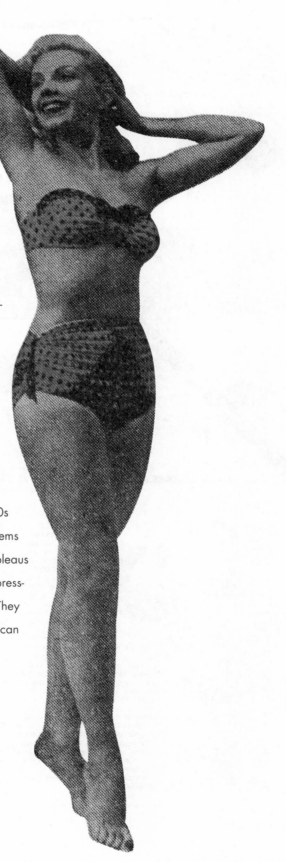

I Can Make YOU a New Man, Too, In Only 15 Minutes a Day!

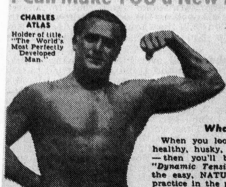

CHARLES ATLAS
Holder of title, "The World's Most Perfectly Developed Man."

PEOPLE used to laugh at my skinny 97-pound body. I was ashamed to strip for sports or for a swim. Girls made fun of me behind my back. THEN I discovered my body-building system, "*Dynamic Tension.*" It made me such a *complete* specimen of manhood that I hold the title, "The World's Most Perfectly Developed Man."

What's My Secret?

When you look in the mirror and see a healthy, husky, fellow smiling back at you — then you'll be astonished at how fast "*Dynamic Tension*" GETS RESULTS! It is the easy, NATURAL method and you can practice in the privacy of your own room — JUST 15 MINUTES EACH DAY. Just watch your scrawny chest and shoulder muscles begin to swell ... those spindly arms and legs of yours bulge ... and your whole body starts to feel "alive," full of zip and go!

Thousands are becoming husky — my way. I give you no gadgets to fool with. With "*Dynamic Tension*" you simply utilize the dormant muscle-power in your own body — watch it grow and multiply into real, solid **LIVE MUSCLE.**

FREE My 32-Page Illustrated Book is Yours — Not for $1.00 or 10c — But FREE

Send for my book, *Everlasting Health and Strength.* 32 pages of photos, valuable advice. Shows what *Dynamic Tension* can do, answers vital questions. A *real prize* for any fellow who wants a better build. I'll send you a copy FREE. It may change your whole life. Rush coupon to me personally: *Charles Atlas, Dept. 33012, 115 E. 23rd Street, New York 10, N. Y.*

have some *real fun* and *sure 'nuff action*
with the
F-500 *Fury*
CAP MACHINE GUN

FIRES 500 SHOTS on a continuous roll of caps

SMOKING ACTION — smoke puffs from the barrel as you let 'er go

MAKES REALISTIC SOUND with or without the caps

FULLY AUTOMATIC — uses ordinary flashlight batteries... no winding or cranking

SUPER FAST SPEED — have twice as much fun as you play

OUTER SPACE DESIGNS are embossed on the sides to add to the fun

Plus an opportunity to win a **FREE TRIP** for three to **Disneyland** HOLLYWOOD, and **PACIFIC OCEAN PARK**; a personal TV set; or silver dollars in Nichols' big **DESIGN A NEW TOY CONTEST** — get the details at your toy dealer

NEW 500-SHOT CAP PISTOL...
trigger it ... cock it ... or fan it! You have more shots and more fun than any other cowboy when you have the Mustang. The special bright finish and plastic staghorn grips are beautiful.

MUSTANG

Wonderful Circle N Toys from
Ⓝ NICHOLS Industries, Inc.
CIRCLE N RANCH   JACKSONVILLE, TEXAS

PIMPLES
dry up in 3 days
OR YOUR MONEY BACK!

At last science has discovered a fast, harmless way to clear your skin of those horrible pimples, blackheads and acne spots. This is an entirely new, greaseless cream that contains powerful A and D vitamins. It works fast by drying out the superfluous skin oils pimples feed on...at the same time counteracts by antiseptic action, the growth of bacteria that cause and spread ugly skin blemishes.

IMPROVE YOUR APPEARANCE
WITH <u>FIRST</u> APPLICATION

You look better the minute you apply wonder-working CLEAR-X, because its amazing skin color hides the blemishes while its medicinal action gets to work clearing them up fast. You don't risk a penny. Get CLEAR-X by sending in the coupon now, use it for 3 days, and if your skin troubles are not definitely improved, you pay nothing.

READER'S DIGEST reports amazing results from the CLEAR-X type of treatment. Experiments by a great medical college on 100 men, women and young people showed improvements in every case.

FREE IF YOU ACT NOW!

A $3.00 jar of CLEAR-X medicated soap to help CLEAR-X work even faster with double action. That's a $6.00 value for just $2.98.

LOVE CAN BE YOURS AGAIN!

You can't blame him (or her) for not wanting to kiss you if your skin is oily, defaced with ugly pimples, blackheads and acne spots. Give yourself a break! CLEAR-X will clear your skin like magic!

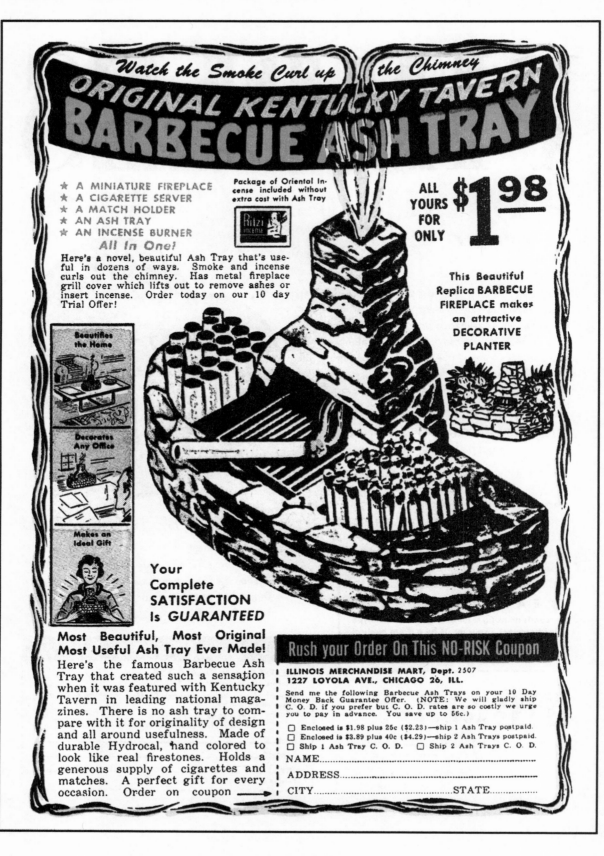

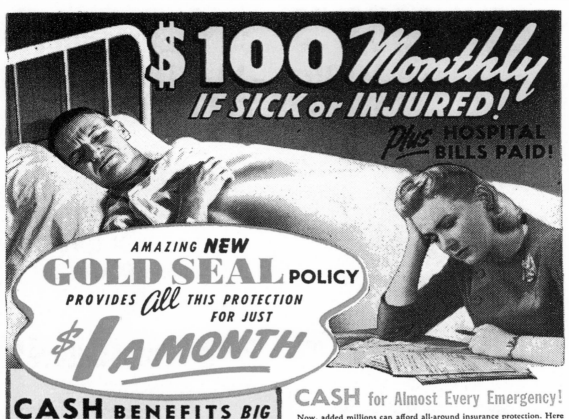

NEW! 1953 "Space Commander"
VIBRO - MATIC
WALKIE-TALKIES

2 PHONES ONLY $1

2 WAY
SENDS! RECEIVES!
VOICE - SONGS - MUSIC

Thrills & Fun Galore!

If by some magical means you could talk with your neighbor and friends—without electric wires, without batteries or electric current, wouldn't you pay $100 or more? Well you can do just that and the entire cost to you is only ONE DOLLAR for TWO "Space Commander" Walkie-Talkies. Not just a toy—but an amazing communication system. NOW you can talk back and forth from house to garden, between rooms, between your house and your friends'. How thrilling to "speak thru space"!

Works like Magic . . . Guaranteed!

This latest, newest 1953 model is a well made product of the world's largest manufacturer of Walkie-Talkies. Uses highly sensitive Vibromatic design. Each phone is self-contained and sends as well as receives messages, songs, music, etc. which travel over the conductor line for hundreds of feet, clear and distinct. Requires no license. Will not interfere with radio reception. Works equally well indoors or out.

Endless Fun . . . Educational!

This new 2-WAY WalkieTalkie System provides endless fun for the entire family, for boys and girls and adults too! Inspirational. Helps overcome shyness, aids voice training. Real "Space Planet" design in handsome colors. Hard to break. They're rugged!

5 Day Trial — Money Back Guarantee.

Send only one dollar, cash, check or money order and your Walkie-Talkies will be shipped on 5 day home trial—instantly! Easy to use directions—even a 5-year-old child can do it! Enjoy them with your family and friends for 5 whole days free of any obligation to keep them . . . entirely at our risk! If you're not thrilled and satisfied in every way your dollar comes right back! Supply limited! Rush order now! Don't lose this big bargain! Mail coupon TODAY!

CONSUMERS MART, Dept. 191-H-28
131 West 33rd Street, New York 1, N. Y.

SPECIAL!
$1
2 PHONES COMPLETE

SENSATIONAL! STARTLING! NEW!

"INVISIBLE HELMET"

PUT IT ON . . .

NOW — YOU SEE PEOPLE — THEY CAN'T SEE YOU!

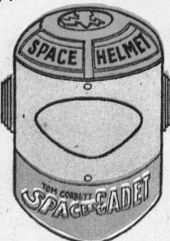

You've GOT to own this! It works like magic! Put on this helmet and nobody can see your face. But you can see everything.

This is a sensational discovery —as new as the Hydrogen Bomb —as exciting as a ride through space — as thrilling an experience as you will ever have!

Helmet is light, unbreakable. You'll say it's miraculous—and it's only $1.98 sent right to your home postpaid! SPECIAL! Two helmets for $3.75.

TOM CORBETT SPACE CADET
COSMIC VISION
HELMET

No one will be able to recognize you when you wear this official space helmet, but you can see them because this helmet has the new mysterious cosmic vision.

Everybody will want one of these helmets and no wonder. Think what you can do with it! Think of how you can fool your friends! Think of how you can put it on and not be recognized and yet how you can see everybody else and what they are doing. If you order now you can get your helmet right away and **BE FIRST IN YOUR NEIGHBORHOOD** to wear it. You will be envied by everyone and you will be having all the fun. Order immediately for quick delivery.

EMPIRE MDSG. CO., Dept. HJ-5
63 Central Ave., Ossining, N. Y.

Don't be disappointed, send now! Use coupon below to order. Only $1.98 each two helmets for $3.75. Sorry, no C.O.D.'s.

EMPIRE MDSG. CO., Dept. **HJ-5**
63 Central Ave., Ossining, N. Y.
Please send me Cosmic Vision Helmet, price_____$1.98
Send TWO Cosmic Vision Helmets for _____$3.75
I enclose cash ☐ check ☐ money order ☐.

Name_____
Address_____
City_____ Zone_____ State_____
SATISFACTION GUARANTEED—OR YOUR MONEY BACK
SORRY, NO C.O.D.'s

-1953-

"I gained 60 lbs. of muscles."

says John Sill

1

HOW TO MOLD A
MIGHTY CHEST
BY GEORGE F. JOWETT

ALL **5** BIG BOOKS YOURS! COUNT THEM!

"I added 7 inches to my CHEST 3 inches to each ARM," says Jobie Jackson

2

W TO MOLD A
GHTY ARM
GEORGE F. JOWETT

Do as I Did

4

HOW TO MOLD A
MIGHTY GRIP
By GEORGE F. JOWETT

3

O MOLD A
GHTY BACK

5

HOW TO MOLD
MIGHTY LEGS

Try For A Free $280 Art Course!

5 PRIZES! 5 Complete $280 Art Courses, including Drawing Outfits!

Draw the girl and try for a prize! Find out if you have profitable art talent. You've nothing to lose—*everything to gain.* Mail your drawing today!

Amateurs Only! Our students not eligible. Make copy of girl 5 ins. high. Pencil or pen only. Omit lettering. All drawings must be received by Dec. 31, 1952. None returned. Winners notified.

BONUS FOR **PROMPTNESS!**
Mail drawing in next 5 days—we'll send you valuable folder on How to Start In Commercial Art—FREE!

ART INSTRUCTION, INC., Dept. 10502-1
500 S. 4th, Minneapolis 15, Minn.
Please enter my attached drawing in your December drawing contest. (PLEASE PRINT)

Name_____ Age_____

Address_____ Phone_____

City_____ Zone____County_____

State_____ Occupation_____

HEY FELLOWS! FIREWORKS

Look What You Get for Only $4.95 from Famous BANNER

THE FIREWORKS CENTER OF AMERICA

A $14.70 VALUE

For ONLY $4.95

Yes sir fellows, this year **BANNER** offers you a selection greater than ever before at the old price of only $4.95. Like everything else the cost of fireworks has gone up. But because you have faithfully year after year continued to buy your fireworks from **BANNER**, it has enabled us to increase our capacity, offer you a greater selection, a greater value, without increasing our price to you. In addition to all your old favorites this selection contains the newest creations in Fireworks.

PRE-TESTED FIREWORKS

Remember every piece of fireworks from **BANNER** must first pass the Famous **BANNER** test for noise, beauty and sure-firing. When you buy from Famous **BANNER** you get **SALUTES** that sound like a bursting shell. **BOMBS** that burst like crash of thunder. **FIRECRACKERS** with a deafening bang. **ROCKETS** that are more beautiful. **CANDLES** that amaze with their beauty as they burst in the air. **BLOCK BUSTERS** that are heard for blocks. **SIREN AERIAL BOMBS** that screech as they zip through the air and explode with a thundering noise. **BATTLE IN THE CLOUDS** they fight it out high in the air. **ZIG ZAG WHISTLES** that whistle and scream as they race madly around. That's the kind of beauty and action you get when you buy your fireworks from **BANNER.**

ORDER EARLY—BE SURE

Get your order in now and avoid the rush that is sure to come later. Fill out the convenient coupon today, or write on a piece of paper the number of assortments you want (1 or more) Sign your name and address and enclose Money Order or Certified Check for full amount. (No C O D Shipments.) All fireworks are sent Express.

Send for This Big New Color Catalog—It's FREE

FIREWORKS Wholesale Prices DIRECT TO YOU FREE

QUICK ACTION ORDER BLANK

BANNER FIREWORKS CORPORATION, DEPT. U-67
446 Capistrano   Toledo 12, Ohio

Enclosed find_____ Send me_____ of your

De Luxe assortments by Express F.O.B. Toledo

Name_____

Street_____

City_____ State_____

Express Office if different from above_____

BANNER FIREWORKS CORPORATION • Dept. U-67
446 CAPISTRANO   **TOLEDO 12, OHIO**

MOON - Glo

In Rich,
Crease-Resistant
Silky Jersey

YOU'LL look like Cinderella in her gayest moment in this dramatic dress. The deep neckline with its gorgeous flower will express your charm, the smart wide self-belt with eyelets will trim your delicate waist and the full, FULL accordion-pleated skirt will make you swing like a balle-rina. Superbly made of rich crease-resist-ant SILKY JERSEY

IN BLACK, WHITE
NAVY, CORAL
and VIOLET

Only
$6.98

Sizes: 11 to 17
12 to 20
16½ to 24½

SEND NO MONEY • 10 DAY FREE TRIAL

Make Your
LAMPS
into **CHRISTMAS TREES**

cleverest decorating idea in years!

Now you can bring Hollywood's famous "Christmas Tree Lane" right into your home. These perfect replicas fit over any lamp in place of your regular shade.. Make all your lamps into Christmas trees and spread the Holiday Spirit throughout your house. Ideal for children's room, window decoration, small apartments, etc. Beautifully lithographed in forest green with white "snow" on branches that stand out for easy decorating. Can be used for many years. Complete with simple illustrated instructions. At this low price you'll want several. Order now . . . Sorry, No C.O.D.'s

17 inches high 17 inches diameter

only $**1**00
postpaid

FREE →
With each order of 2 or more shades, you'll receive FREE a 12-page book of the world's most popular Hymns and Carols . . . words and music.

CLIP AND MAIL

XMAS TREE LAMPSHADES Dept. X-211
114 East 32 St., New York 16, N. Y.

Please send me _____ Xmas Tree Lampshades for which I enclose $_____

Check ☐ Cash ☐ Money Order ☐

Name _____

Address _____

City_____ Zone_____ State_____

KILL THESE HAIR-DESTROYING GERMS
WITH WARD'S FORMULA

PITYROSPORUM OVALE · MICROCOCCUS · STAPHYLOCOCCUS ALBUS · MICROBACILLUS

SCALP ITCH · FALLING HAIR · DANDRUFF · HEAD ODORS

NOTHING, Absolutely nothing known to Science can do more to
SAVE YOUR HAIR

Beware of your itchy scalp, hair loss, dandruff, head scales, unpleasant head odors! Nature may be warning you of approaching baldness. Heed Nature's warning! Treat your scalp to scientifically prepared Ward's Formula.

Millions of trouble-breeding bacteria, living on your sick scalp (see above) are killed on contact. Ward's Formula kills not one, but *all four* types of these destructive scalp germs now recognized by many medical authorities as a significant cause of baldness. Kill these germs—don't risk letting them kill your hair growth.

ENJOY THESE 5 BENEFITS IMMEDIATELY

1. Kills these 4 types of germs that retard normal hair growth—*on contact*
2. Removes ugly infectious dandruff—*fast*
3. Brings hair-nourishing blood to scalp—*quickly*
4. Stops annoying scalp itch and burn—*instantly*
5. Starts wonderful self-massaging action—*within 3 seconds*

Once you're bald, that's *it*, friends! There's nothing you can do. Your hair is gone forever. So are your chances of getting it back. But Ward's Formula, used as directed, keeps your sick scalp free of itchy dandruff, seborrhea, and stops the hair loss they cause. Almost at once your hair looks thicker, more attractive and alive.

We don't ask you to believe *us*. Thousands of men and women—first skeptical just as you are—have *proved* what we say. Read *their* grateful letters. Study the guarantee—it's *better* than a free trial! Then try Ward's Formula at *our* risk. Use it for only 10 short days. You must enjoy *all* the benefits we claim—or we return not only the price you pay—but DOUBLE YOUR MONEY BACK. You be the judge! © Ward Laboratories Inc.,19 West 44th St., New York 36, N. Y.

TO SAVE YOUR HAIR ACT NOW
Send coupon today for 10-day offer. Send No Money

Proof!
We get letters like these every day from grateful men and women all over the world.

I must admit I didn't have much faith in it, but I hadn't been using Ward's one week before I could see it was helping me. I could feel my hair getting thicker.
E. K., Cleveland, Ohio

Out of all the Hair Experts I went to, I've gotten the *most* help from one bottle of Ward's Formula.
C. La M., Philadelphia, Pa.

After using Ward's for only 12 days, my hair has stopped falling out.
R. W. C., Cicero, Ill.

I am tickled to death with the results. In just two weeks' time—no dandruff! *W. T. W., Portola, Cal.*

I feel encouraged to say that the infuriating scalp itch which has bothered me for 5 years is now gone.
J. M. K., Columbus, Ohio

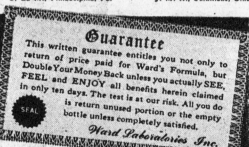

Guarantee
This written guarantee entitles you not only to return of price paid for Ward's Formula, but Double Your Money Back unless you actually SEE, FEEL and ENJOY all benefits herein claimed in only ten days. The test is at our risk. All you do is return unused portion or the empty bottle unless completely satisfied.
Ward Laboratories Inc.

SFAL

——ACT TODAY or YOU MAY BE TOO LATE!——

Ward Laboratories Inc.,
19 West 44th St., **6111-F,** New York 36, N. Y.

Rush Ward's Formula to me at once. I will pay postman two dollars plus postage. I must be completely satisfied within 10 days, or you GUARANTEE refund of DOUBLE MY MONEY BACK upon return of bottle and unused portion.

Name ....
Address ....
City .... Zone....... State.............

☐ Check here if you enclose $2.00 with order, and we will pay postage. Same refund offer holds, of course.

APO, FPO, Canada & Foreign add 50c; no C.O.D.s.

DOUBLE YOUR MONEY BACK GUARANTEE

-1954-

37

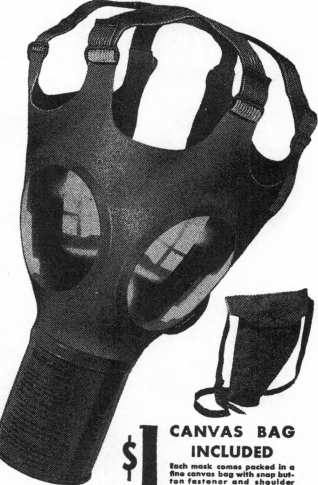

-1946-

...rties of gifts. Fun
dren and adults alike.

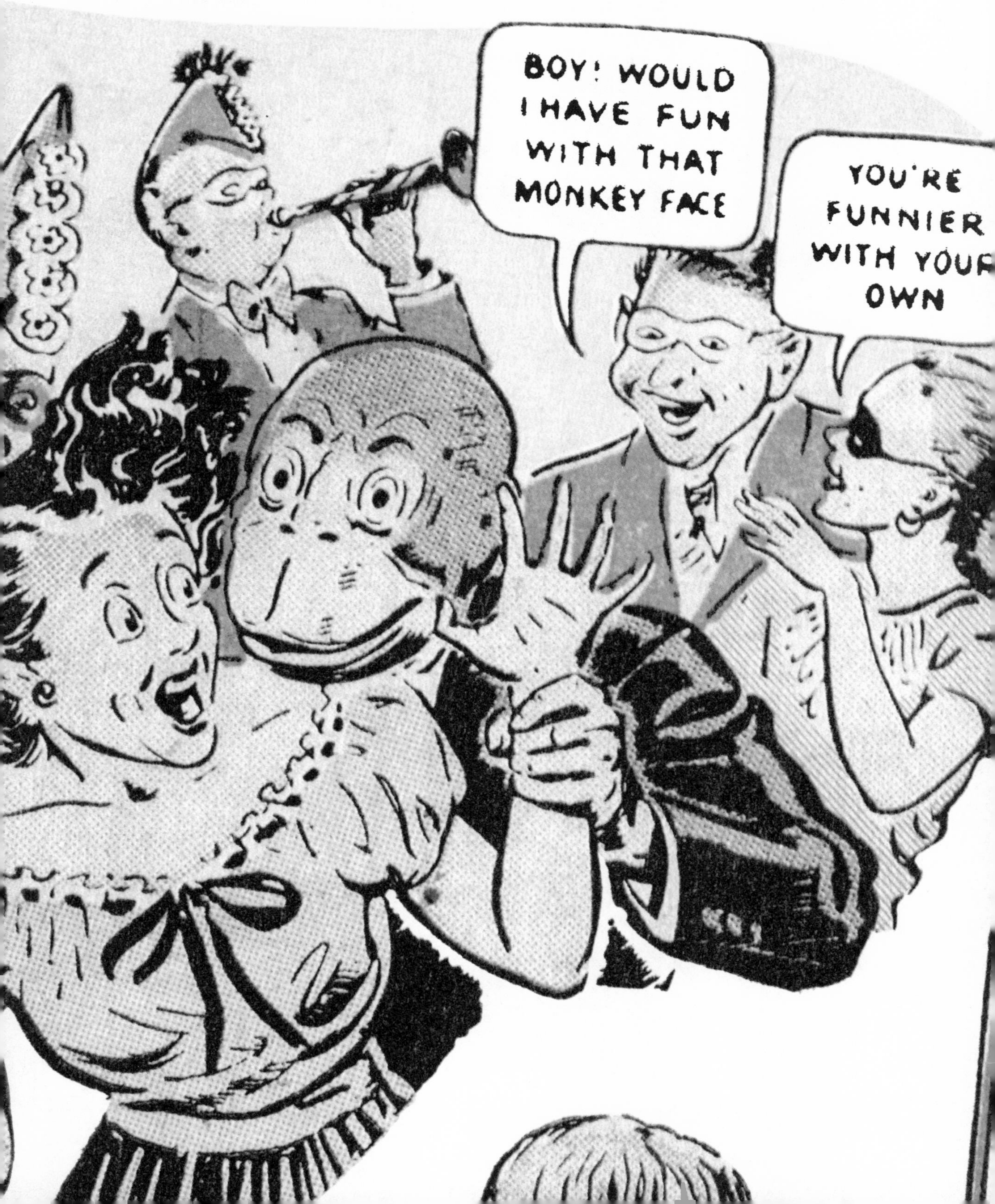

-1946-

43

-1946-

SPECIAL...
INTRODUCTORY OFFER
to Readers of This Magazine

ALL-IN-ONE CIGARETTE LIGHTER and FULL-PACK CASE
Personalized with Your Name

FOR MEN AND WOMEN

HINGED LID

YOUR NAME

Only $1.98
Your Name Engraved in 23 Karat Gold without Extra Cost

NEW! IMPROVED!

All-in-One Cigarette Lighter and Full-Pack Case gives you a cigarette and a light—BOTH at the same time! Smart, streamlined and modern. This wonderful convenience is compact . . . fits easily in your pocket or purse. No more tobacco crumbs. No more bent or damp cigarettes. Insures lasting freshness. Deep well lighter holds an amazingly large supply of fluid. Built for lifetime service of beautiful mottled plastic. Only lighter case with hinged lid. Opens with a snap of your finger. Your name engraved on case in 23 Karat gold letters. An ideal gift for men or women. Order Now.

SEND NO MONEY
Use 10 Days At Our Risk

Just mail name and address for trial inspection and approval. On arrival deposit $1.98 plus C.O.D. postage. Use 10 days. If not delighted return for refund of purchase price. (Send cash, H & S Sales Co. pays postage.)

EXTRA FOR PROMPT ACTION... If you order now, we will engrave any name in 23 Karat gold without extra cost. Order now for yourself or as a gift for someone else.

Dept. 130 • **H. & S. SALES CO.** • 1665 Milwaukee Ave. • Chicago 47, Ill.

CLIP AND MAIL COUPON NOW

H. & S. SALES CO.,
1665 Milwaukee Ave., Chicago 47, Ill.   Dept. 130

Please rush combination cigarette case and lighter. I will pay postman only $1.98 plus C.O.D. postage on arrival. I may return in 10 days for refund of purchase price if not delighted. (Send cash, H & S Sales Co. pays postage.)

NAME _____

ADDRESS _____

CITY _____ ZONE _____ STATE _____

NAME TO BE ENGRAVED _____
(Print Plainly)

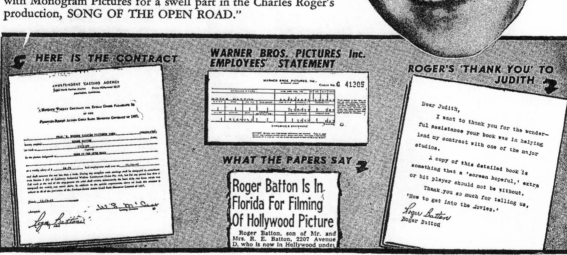

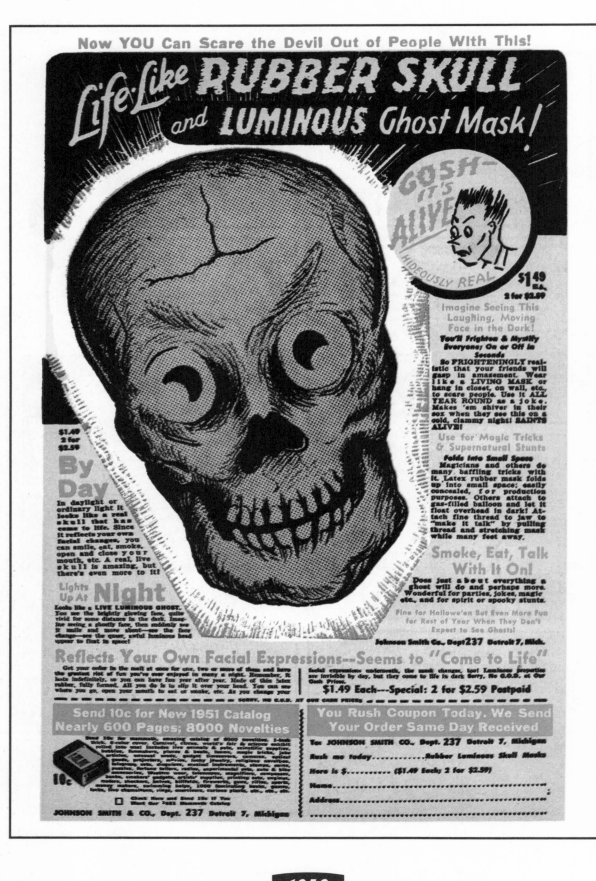

10 POWER TELESCOPE

Here's The Only FULL 10-POWER Telescope At This Price In America Today

It's Precision Built! Makes Far Away Objects Stand Out Clear—Sharp—BIG AS LIFE!

Here's the only full 10-POWER Telescope being offered in America today at the unheard-of low price of only 98c. Easily the most outstanding telescope value you'll find anywhere. You'd expect to pay up to $10.00 and more for such power. And anyone who knows telescopes will tell you a good 10-Power telescope is worth all of that. But now, due to a fortunate purchase, we are able to offer you this 10-POWER Precision-built Telescope at a sensational bargain. Don't confuse it with small "weak-vision" telescopes. This one is high-powered and measures a full 16 inches. The lenses are of fine optically-ground polished glass—a product of one of America's leading optical houses. The case is durable and extends easily. Focuses instantly on stationary or moving objects—brings them 10 times closer. With the country at war, everybody needs a telescope like this—to spot airplanes, to identify distant objects, to bring into sharp, easy vision people, animals, signs, houses—which may be beyond the range of the naked eye. Valuable to Air Wardens, Boy Scouts, Sailors, Sportsmen. Ideal for fights, ball games, races, outdoor events. However, hurry! There's no telling how long we can continue to supply this precision-built 10-POWER Telescope at this amazingly low price. Once our present limited supply is gone, we cannot repeat this offer again.

CLIP COUPON BELOW and MAIL TODAY!

Just clip the coupon to the left below and mail with only 98c (plus 10c for the packing and postage). If you want two telescopes send only $1.79 plus 10c. You take no risk. Use the telescope for 10 full days. Focus it on objects miles away. Have your friends try it. Convince yourself that here is a telescope anyone would be thrilled to have—one you'll be proud to own. If after 10 days' trial you're not positively delighted with the way this powerful telescope helps you to see great distances, we ask you to return it without delay and we will refund your money in full, no questions asked. Remember, the supply is limited—so hurry!

Only 98¢

BRINGS OBJECTS 10 TIMES CLOSER

FREE!

Rush the above order coupon at once and we will also include FREE a valuable Airplane Spotter's Chart showing 31 Allied and Axis planes. Helps you to easily identify these planes.

MEASURES FULL 16 INCHES IN LENGTH

AMAZING NEW GAME Sensation "LET'S GO TO COLLEGE"

The Newest COAST-to-COAST CRAZE

Panic a party

You'll want one to make your home parties a riot of fun. Also an ideal holiday gift. Send your order today; only $1 postpaid.

Once in a Blue Moon comes a game like this. Fascinating! Grows on everybody! Panics a party! By Christmas—the fad of the nation! Your friends have an unforgettable good time. Brings together excitement of rolling dice, the fun of rummy, interspersed with the rah-rah spirit of College Life.

Every throw of the dice attracts attention, and the result affects all players. Each player rolls the dice to pass his courses. Hilarious incidents of Sports, Fun, Re-exam and Flunk cards keep the game full of pep from start to finish. The player with the best hand at end of game is the winnah!

Friend or Foe?

You Can Tell at Once With the Amazing New 2-Line
FLASH IDENTIFICATION SYSTEM Found Only in the

AIRCRAFT SPOTTERS' HANDBOOK

Identifies 350 Bombers, Fighters, Transports and Other Aircraft of
Warring Nations. Over 1,300 Photos and 3-Position Silhouettes,
with Descriptions, Specifications and Recognition Characteristics.

Size 5½ x 7"

THE most comprehensive, up-to-the-minute Aircraft Spotters' Handbook in America! Includes hundreds more fighting aircraft than any
other similar manual! Amazing new *2-line* FLASH IDENTIFICA-
TION feature is practically a course in aircraft-spotting! Recognition
Characteristics are listed by the famous WEFT Formula—*Wings, Engines, Fuselage,* and *Tail*—for easy comparison. Helps you distinguish
friendly and enemy planes at a glance. 350 military aircraft are de-
scribed and illustrated, including nearly 100 American warplanes, over
60 British, 60 German, 35 Jap, 40 Italian, as well as planes of Russia,
Netherlands, Norway, Spain, France. Includes also Barrage Balloons,
Blimps, Gliders, and Rotating Wing Aircraft. Photographs! Specifications! Markings! Silhouette views from three angles!

Many authorities expect air attacks here at any time and urge thorough preparation on the part of citizens. Civilian aircraft spotters can
render valuable patriotic service with the help of this Handbook.

You'll also be able to identify all the famous planes you read about
in the news—American Flying Fortresses, Liberators and Thunder-
bolts; British Hurricanes and Spitfires; Russian Stormoviks and Mos-
cas; German Focke-Wulfs and Messerschmitts; Jap Zeros; and hundreds more! Over 1,500,000 of our Spotters' Guides have been bought
by the U. S. Armed Forces and Civilians. This complete Handbook combines all four guides, plus valuable new material and the *2-line* Flash Identification.

Sturdy, flexible, water-repellent binding patterned
on lines similar to the official U. S. Army Drill Manuals. Handy THUMB INDEXING. *Quantity limited.* Rush order on coupon below. National Aeronautics Council, Inc., 37 West 47th St., New York
19, N. Y. (Copyright, 1943, by National Aeronautics Council, Inc.)

The Most Authoritative Book of Its Kind in the World!

$1.00 only

384 pages! a $4 value

hensive Handbook is a practical guide for everyone interested in avia-
tion—as a career or hobby, or for military service. Experts have checked
and rechecked every picture, dimension, description and specification
that it is permissible to publish: span, length, height, gross weight,
maximum speed, cruising range; type of plane, engines—with number
and horsepower, wings, fuselage, tail—including fin and rudder, con-
struction, armament, landing gear; country, model, name, markings;
bomb load capacity, etc. Edited by L. C. Guthman, Ensign, U. S. N. R.

HOW THE *2-LINE* FLASH
IDENTIFICATION WORKS

The two planes below look very much alike, although one's a
Nazi and the other American. But any youngster can instantly
tell them apart with the *2-line* FLASH IDENTIFICATION.

Aeronautics Photo

Airpix, Toronto

Long-Nosed Fuselage Suspended on Wings.
Twin Tail Booms. Rounded Tail Plane.

Short-Nosed Fuselage Suspended on Wings.
Twin Tail Booms. Rectangular Tail Plane.

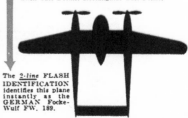

The *2-line* FLASH
IDENTIFICATION
identifies this plane
instantly as the
AMERICAN Lock-
heed P-38 Light-
ning.

The *2-line* FLASH
IDENTIFICATION
identifies this plane
instantly as the
GERMAN Focke-
Wulf FW. 189.

56

-1957-

DRAW for COMIC BOOKS

Learn and earn in your spare time... at HOME!!

HUNDREDS OF NEW COMIC BOOKS ON SALE HAVE CREATED A TERRIFIC DEMAND FOR ARTISTS! NOW, A COMIC ILLUSTRATION COURSE HAS BEEN PERSONALLY PREPARED BY PROFESSIONAL COMIC BOOK ARTISTS! -- TO ENABLE *YOU* TO BECOME A PROFESSIONAL COMIC BOOK ARTIST *YOURSELF!* NORMAN MAURER AND JOE KUBERT, THE MEN WHO PRODUCED THE WORLD'S FIRST 3-D COMIC BOOK, WILL TEACH *YOU* TO DRAW FOR COMIC BOOKS!

HI - I'M JOE KUBERT. IN THESE ART LESSONS, I'LL SHOW YOU HOW TO DRAW *STRAIGHT STYLE* OR *ADVENTURE COMICS!* NORMAN AND I WILL GIVE YOU *HUNDREDS* OF IMPORTANT PROFESSIONAL TIPS -- THINGS THAT WE'VE LEARNED DURING THE 30 YEARS WE'VE BEEN IN THE COMIC BOOK BUSINESS!

I'M NORMAN MAURER. MY SECTION OF THE ART LESSONS WILL SHOW HOW TO DRAW *COMIC STYLE* OR *HUMOROUS COMICS!* OUR LESSONS WILL ALSO TELL YOU HOW TO WRITE, LETTER AND COLOR FOR COMIC BOOKS. YOU CAN LEARN BY PRACTICING AS LITTLE AS 15 MINUTES A DAY -- *IN YOUR OWN HOME!*

TALENT IS *NOT* NECESSARY! THE *DESIRE TO DRAW* IS *IMPORTANT!!* THIS COMIC BOOK ILLUSTRATORS INSTRUCTION COURSE GIVES YOU ALL THE *INSIDE SECRETS!* SIMPLE LESSONS MAKE LEARNING A JOY! EASY TO UNDERSTAND AS A COMIC BOOK ITSELF! NEW, NOVEL TEACHING TECHNIQUE MAY ENABLE YOU TO DRAW REAL COMIC-TYPE FIGURES IN A MATTER OF *MINUTES!* ENROLLMENT LIMITED! ACT *NOW!*

mail this TODAY!

GET COMPLETE FIRST LESSON FOR ONLY $1.00 ! ON OUR MONEY-BACK GUARANTEE *OR* ASK FOR *FREE* INFORMATION!

TO: **SCHOLART INSTITUTE**
P.O. BOX 787, DEPT. T-354
BEVERLY HILLS, CALIFORNIA

☐ I AM ANXIOUS TO START IMMEDIATELY. *RUSH* LESSON #1 TO ME. ENCLOSED, FIND $1.00 IN CASH, CHECK OR MONEY ORDER. MONEY RETURNED IN 10 DAYS IF I'M NOT *COMPLETELY SATISFIED!*

☐ SEND *FREE INFORMATION* ON COMIC BOOK ILLUSTRATORS INSTRUCTION COURSE. I ASSUME NO OBLIGATION!

NAME _____

STREET _____

CITY _____

ZONE _____ STATE _____

giant inflatable toys of pre-historic monsters who ruled the earth millions of years ago

7 GIGANTIC DINOSAURS

WITH GENUINE TOSS-UP FEET ACTION!

MOLDED ONE-PIECE QUALITY LATEX!

COMPLETELY INFLATABLE!

for $1.00

(No COD's please)

up to 4 FEET TALL

Here's thrilling excitement for everyone with this giant-size collection of pre-historic dinosaurs at this low, low price of just $1.00 (plus post.) Thrill to their fascinating names! Command these fun-loving pre-historic monsters to your every prank! Toss them in the air and they always land on their feet . . . swinging and swaying in every direction without tilting over. Great for children! Terrific for parties! Colossal for adults! So order right now for stupendous fun. Fill out the coupon below. You take no risk because you must agree that these giant dinosaurs are everything we say or your money promptly refunded.

THEY SWING AND SWAY IN EVERY DIRECTION!

THEY BEND, LEAN AND TILT!

EVEN THE TINIEST BREEZE ANIMATES THEM!

THEY BOUNCE AND HOP!

THEY STAND AND WIGGLE!

7 DIFFERENT PRE-HISTORIC MONSTERS IN EACH PACKAGE

CERATOSAURUS

TRACHODON

TYRANNOSAURUS REX

SEA SERPENT

ARMORED DEMIHTHYS

PROSAUROLOPHUS

ALLOSAURUS

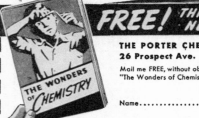

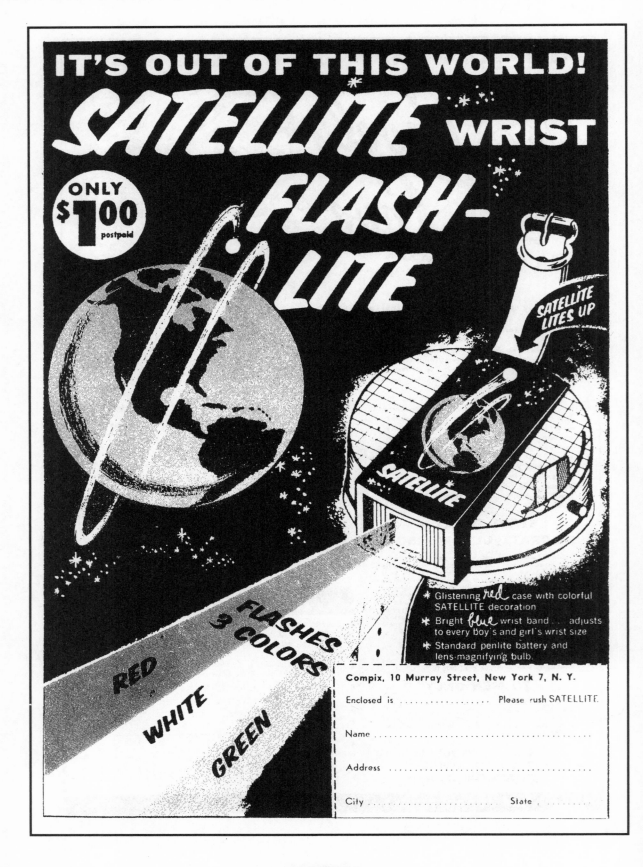

66

EXCITING ANT FARM

FASCINATING!

A living TV screen. The ants put on a quiet but exciting show that will keep you fascinated for hours.

EDUCATIONAL!

An education in nature study as well as work and patience.

ONLY $2.98

Watch them dig tunnels — see them build rooms — marvel as they erect bridges and move mountains before your very eyes. Ants are the world's tiniest engineers . . . and seeing them plan and construct their intricate highways and subways is fascinating. But they do much more than that! Through the clear plastic walls of your ANT FARM you can see the ant soldiers guarding the roads . . . the laborers carrying their loads . . . the supply corps storing away food for the rest of the colony.

FREE BOOK!

"The Ant Watcher's Manual!" is included with every ANT FARM. It tells you all about your ants and what to expect of them.

HERE'S AN ANT'S ENTIRE WORLD!

Thousands Sold at this LOW PRICE!

LIFETIME CHRONOGRAPH
STOPWATCH — WINDOW CALENDAR
WRIST-WATCH *PRECISION JEWELED*

Comes with Handsome Matching Expansion Band AT NO EXTRA COST! WEAR AND ENJOY This Watch on

DATE CHANGES EVERY DAY *Auto-matically*

10-DAY FREE TRIAL!

This Swiss-Precision Watch is Also a

- **TACHOMETER:** Measures speeds of moving objects.
- **TELEMETER:** Measures distance between points.

and

- **12 HOUR RECORDER**

It's Also **ANTI-MAGNETIC**

ONLY $8.95 plus 10% Fed. Tax

1-YEAR GUARANTEE Against defective workmanship and materials. A Lifetime Service Guarantee after one year period. Watch will be serviced and repaired at the cost of parts only, our labor free.

A sensational bargain! Don't miss it — or you may be too late! You have always wanted a watch with these expensive features Now you can have them AT A PRICE YOU CAN AFFORD! This accurate, precision-made Window Calendar Chronograph is ideal for the members of our Armed Services, for sportsmen, doctors, photographers, engineers, technicians, executives, etc. And as for gifts. it's A PERFECT GIFT FOR EVERY OCCASION, such as Graduation, Birthday, Anniversary, Holiday, etc. SEND NO MONEY! Simply mail coupon below for 10-Day FREE TRIAL. Do it now, before supply is exhausted!

Check These Features!

THESE HIGH PRICE FEATURES USUALLY OFFERED IN WATCHES SELLING AT $50.00 or MORE

- Precision Made, Imported Swiss Jeweled Movement.
- 2-Push Buttons for "Stop" and "Start."
- Red Sweep-Second Hand.
- Unbreakable Crystal.
- Triple Chrome-Plated Case for Lasting Wear.

- Chronograph, Window Calendar and Stopwatch All-in-One.
- Radium Glow See-At-Night Hands and Numerals.
- Anti-Magnetic.
- Handsome, Matching Expansion Wristband.

How-to-use, complete instructions plus 1-Year Guarantee and Lifetime Service Guarantee included.

MONEY-BACK GUARANTEE!

Be sure to order this amazing Chronograph Stopwatch — Window Calendar Wrist-Watch WHILE THE SUPPLY LASTS! Use it — and ENJOY IT—for 10 full days. If this wonderful combination timepiece isn't everything we say it is, return it for immediate refund of your purchase price. Don't take a chance on being disappointed ... mail FREE-TRIAL Coupon NOW!

BUYER'S GUILD, Inc., Woodbridge, N. J., Dept. 3111

MAIL FREE-TRIAL COUPON TODAY!

BUYER'S GUILD, Inc., Dept. 3111
Woodbridge, New Jersey

Send _____ Chronograph Watch(es) at $8.95 plus 90¢ Fed. Tax each. I enclose $1 for each watch. Will pay postman balance, plus postage. If not completely satisfied may return Watch within 10 days for immediate refund of purchase price.

Name_____

Address_____

City & Zone_____ State_____

☐ SAVE POSTAGE! Send $9.85 (includes Fed. Tax) and we pay postage. Same 10-Day Free Trial and Money-Back Guarantee

Just Follow the Instructions in This Amazing New Book!

No longer will your letters be dry, awkward and uninteresting. HOW TO WRITE LOVE LETTERS shows you how the most common things can sound interesting—will help you express your personality in your letters. This new book contains dozens of actual sample letters that show just how to write love letters from beginning to end. Included are scores of model love letters by world-famous people—lists of useful synonyms—common errors, and how to avoid them—the correct spelling of many catchy words—many other important letter-writing hints. And remember, with each book you receive ONE YEAR'S supply of Gold Monograms for your writing paper, FREE! Stravon Publishers, 342 Madison Avenue, N. Y. C.

MONEY-BACK OFFER!

We believe you can write real love letters that click with the help of this amazing book—but we want *you* to be the judge! Examine the book for 10 days at our expense—if not delighted with results, return it and your money will be promptly refunded!

FREE

with Each Order —One Year's Supply of Gold Monograms for Your STATIONERY!

PARTIAL CONTENTS

How to express your love.
How to make him (or her) miss you.
How to assure him (or her) of your faithfulness.
How to "break the ice."
How to tell your husband (or wife) those "little things" of love.
How to discourage the "too romantic" friend.
How to *propose* by letter.
How to make your sweetheart write more often.
How to write the girl you met on your day off.
How to "make up" with your sweetheart.
How to make everyday events sound interesting.

AND MANY OTHER CHAPTERS!

MEDICAL TABLET DISCOVERY!

SAFE, NEW, EASY WAY !

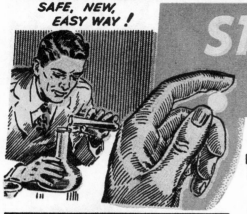

STOPS "BED WETTING"

Without Electrical Devices... Rubber Sheets... Alarms...

Ends Shame, Discomfort, Inconvenience Almost Miraculously!

WHY endure the needless shame, embarrassment, humiliation . . . the discomfort and distress of this unfortunate habit? Why put up with the daily nuisance of changing and washing bed linen and clothes? Why suffer the mortification of foul smelling bedrooms . . . the expense of ruined furniture . . . the danger of catching cold and infectious rashes?

Doctors agree that BED-WETTING can cause nervousness, stuttering and emotional disturbances in children, very often seriously affecting their future and character, making them "psychological cripples."

But now the disgrace and danger of BED-WETTING can very easily be a thing of the past with amazing new DRY-TABS. At last, medical science has discovered a safe, new, easy way to step BED-WETTING without electrical devices . . . without rubber sheets, alarms or special diets and without interrupting needed sleep. DRY-TABS, in easy-to-take tablet form, does away with BED-WETTING as painlessly, easily and simply as swallowing an aspirin. Yes, almost miraculously, amazing, safe DRY-TABS, used as directed, help stop functional BED-WETTING . . . relieve tension and strain, often the underlying cause in most cases of this unfortunate habit. Now, for the first time, safe DRY-TABS can be obtained without prescription.

SIMPLE SAFE TABLET DOES IT

DRY-TABS is the same safe medical discovery that is prescribed by many doctors. Now, it is available for the first time without prescription to all the victims of BED-WETTING who long to rid themselves of this distressing habit once and for all. DRY-TABS is safe, not habit forming, contains no harmful drugs—Follow simple directions.

"DRY-TAB THERAPY" Eventually Allows BED-WETTING Victims to Function Normally Without Further Medication

DRY-TABS, in most cases, does not offer merely temporary stopping of BED-WETTING. In case after case, as revealed in clinical tests conducted in hospitals by medical scientists, the DRY-TABS formula proved itself to be a tablet that gives direct support to the patient in controlling his BED-WETTING. The benefits of the DRY-TABS formula may be expected to be effective beyond the period when it is taken regularly. It helps the BED-WETTING victim to retrain, tends to increase strength of sphincter and detrusor muscles controlling urination. Many cases have discontinued the use of DRY-TABS after a short time and found they were functioning normally. So BED-WETTING victims do not have to be slaves to any kind of medication if their case is of the type that responds to the re-training power of DRY-TABS. This is probably one of the greatest advancements ever made in BED-WETTING therapy. Yes, once DRY-TABS stops BED-WETTING, its use may no longer be required, normal functioning and control may be developed almost miraculously. So don't hesitate a minute longer. Order DRY-TABS Today!

DEVELOPED AFTER YEARS OF EXTENSIVE HOSPITAL AND CLINICAL RESEARCH AS REVEALED IN MEDICAL LITERATURE

The discoveries of science, many times, are brought about by indirect means. Take the case of the exclusive DRY-TABS formula. Medical practitioners chanced upon this formula while they were investigating a remedy for another illness. Noting the remarkable effect that this formula had upon BED-WETTING they concentrated their efforts on this new data and developed the formula to its present state of perfection. The result is the new DRY-TABS, a remarkable tablet that has brought new hope to thousands of tormented victims of BED-WETTING. Before this formula was released to the public, it was tested in clinics and hospitals by medical scientists on controlled groups of patients. The DRY-TABS formula is the result of thorough medical research, the same kind of research and care that is given to any product that is to be placed in the hands of the public. Chalk up BED-WETTING as one more ailment that has been conquered by the men of science. Think of it, no expensive electrical devices, cumbersome rubber sheets, special diets or mechanical alarms. Just a wonderful new tablet . . . DRY-TABS . . . product of medical research . . . offering the hope of a new future for all these sufferers of BED-WETTING. Be sure to order DRY-TABS today!

ADULTS: START LIVING A NORMAL LIFE TONIGHT!

Scientific tests actually prove DRY-TABS to be 75% effective in stopping this unfortunate habit—even after years of torment! Ends the constant worry of overnight hotel stops and fear of public embarrassment while napping on trains and buses. Don't wait another day. If your loved ones suffer the humiliation, the disgrace, insecurity and helplessness only BED-WETTING can cause, order DRY-TABS NOW! Easy to take, can be dissolved in water if necessary. Just follow simple directions.

DRY-TABS Amazing Formula Effective in 75% of Cases

CASE NO. 1. Healthy, intelligent boy, 9 years old. BED-WETTING since infancy. Child could not break habit. All other medication failed. DRY-TABS formula taken for two three-week periods. Child has remained well for the past three years.

CASE NO. 2. Normal boy, history of BED-WETTING since infancy. Child had no organic defect. Various cures failed. Put on DRY-TABS formula regime. After a month, habit suddenly stopped.

CASE NO. 3. Male, aged 23 years. BED-WETTING since birth. Many forms of treatment failed. Unable to accept invitation to sleep out over-night. Recently married, and embarrassed by habit. After formula taken, wet bed the first two nights but never since that time.

CASE NO. 4. Girl, aged 6 years. Wet bed since infancy. Nervous, irritable. DRY-TABS formula administered for regular period. BED-WETTING stopped almost immediately. Slight relapse. Formula administered again. Child responded immediately once more, and history reveals no further relapse.

CASE NO. 5. Man, 42 years old, wet "heavily." Medication started. Wet during second week and continued to wet when medication was withdrawn for following week. Restarted after rest period, and after five-day treatment seemed to retain control of bladder function.

CASE NO. 6. Woman, 76 years old. DRY-TABS formula administered for 6 days. Improvement, upon withdrawal of medication, improvement remained. Continued gradual return of control. One year without formula and control is adequate.

MAKE THIS HOME TEST: Here is your guarantee of satisfaction. Try DRY-TABS for the prescribed period. If you are not completely overjoyed with DRY-TABS' amazing ability to help stop BED-WETTING, your purchase price will be refunded. Accept this no-risk offer. Order DRY-TABS now!

SEND NO MONEY: Just name and address for generous 3-week supply. On arrival pay postman only $3.00 per package plus C.O.D. charges on guarantee of complete satisfaction or money back.

(Printed in the United States of America)

FREE...10 HITLER STAMPS

10 Scarce Stamps – All Different – Sent Free

TO SECURE NAMES FOR OUR MAILING LIST

-1948-

77

Win! Play BINGO AT HOME

Exciting!
Some FUN!

Now play BINGO at home with this fascinating automatic Bingo outfit. You'll get an added kick pushing the levers waiting for your winning numbers to come up.

Size 3½" X 4½"

It's New! Fascinating!

BINGO is a new, attractive way of playing this fascinating game at home or at parties. Many can play at the same time. All will be held in suspense waiting for the matching number on their cards to come up when the plunger is pushed.

Made of nickel-plated polished pressed steel with attractive stripes of dull satin finish. Numbers and letters on dials are large and attractively colored.

Furnished complete with master chart, good supply of BINGO cards and fibre markers . . . sufficient for 15 players. BINGO furnished complete, ready to play, for only $2.98. Pay postman price plus postage or send $3.00 now and we pay postage.

Only $2.98 COMPLETE

Guaranteed
Fully Guaranteed to Please or full refund of purchase price within 5 days.

SEND NO MONEY! RUSH COUPON!

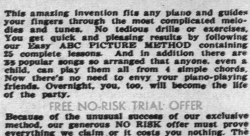

Give Your Kiddie His Own Phonograph

Let Little Folk Play And Enjoy Music!

Sensational PHONO-TOON

PLAYS ANY KIDDIE RECORD UP TO 7 INCH SIZE

BEAUTIFUL UNBREAKABLE RECORDS

ALL PHONO-TOON records are non-breakable . . . a definite necessity for the rough handling you can't prevent kiddies from, especially when they are excited with the joy that comes with PHONO-TOON. You get 5 unbreakable records which include:

"Yankee Doodle"

"Pop Goes the Weasel"

"Polly-Wolly Doodle"

"Mary Had a Little Lamb"

"Twinkle, Twinkle, Little Star"

or other records of our choice.

Today—fill in and mail coupon for PHONO-TOON and five unbreakable records. Order C.O.D. and pay postage on delivery or enclose money now and we'll pay postage. Let your kiddie enjoy the new fun for 10 days. Then if you decide it isn't worth far more than the cost, return for money back. No risk at all—so don't delay. Rush coupon now!

10 DAY FREE TRIAL

MAIL COUPON

Parents! Friends of kiddies! Here's a new thrill and happiness for your favorite little one! PHONO-TOON is a miniature, but a real phonograph. Delightfully plays any kiddie record up to 7 inch size! Hours and hours of fun. Gleeful entertainment listening to kiddie songs with words and music.

EASY TO OPERATE!

PHONO-TOON has been created for kiddies. Therefore, it is simple to change the record and make it play. Durably constructed to protect it from rough handling. Plays beautifully and is attractively designed, with gaily colored Mother Goose reproductions.

$3.98 WITH 5 UNBREAKABLE RECORDS

ALL METAL—STURDILY MADE

PHONO-TOON is sturdily made of all metal. Has no sharp corners. Is safe for any kiddie, regardless of age.

PRACTICAL AND BEAUTIFUL

PHONO-TOON requires no hook-up, no electricity. Nothing to break. Just turn handle for a clear, split-second musical reception. Horn specially made for clear sound and volume. Needle changed by little hands easily and quickly. The smile that won't come off will radiate from your favorite kiddie when enjoying this new musical pleasure!

MAIL THIS COUPON TODAY

FUN INDUSTRIES, DEPT. 509-E
45 East 17th Street, New York City

Rush PHONO-TOON RECORD PLAYER for only $3.98 — with 5 unbreakable records.

☐ Send C.O.D. I will pay C.O.D. parcel post charges, plus handling.
☐ To save postage and handling, I enclose money. Send postpaid.

Name _____

Address _____

City, Zone, State _____

MONEY BACK GUARANTEE: If not delighted with PHONO-TOON and records return in 10 days for full refund of purchase price.

Make Your Own Records

SING! TALK! ACT! PLAY ANY MUSICAL INSTRUMENT!

THINK OF IT! I JUST MADE THIS RECORD WITH THE HOME RECORD MAKER!

IT'S SO SIMPLE! LET ME MAKE A RECORD

GEE BOB, IT WORKS GREAT!

ENJOY MAKING RECORDS IN THE PRIVACY OF YOUR OWN HOME

Now you can make records of your singing, talking, reciting, or instrument playing right in your own home! No longer need the high price of recording machines or studio facilities prevent you or your family from hearing their own voice or playing. *No Experience Necessary.* Set up the NEW HOME RECORD MAKER, play, talk, or sing, and immediately you have a record which you and your friends can enjoy.

D-A-D-D-Y M-O-M-M-Y

Record your child's voice -- catch those precious moments.

MAKE YOUR OWN RECORDS at HOME

IT'S AMAZINGLY SIMPLE!

Make records right in your own home by just singing, talking, acting, or playing a musical instrument into your own record player using a NEW HOME RECORD MAKING UNIT. This wonderful little unit records on the blank records furnished with your recording kit. No processing of the record required . . . just make your recording and it is immediately ready for playback. USE THE NEW HOME RECORD MAKER with most any standard record player — hand winding, portable, radio-phono combination or electrical phonographs operating on either AC or DC.

What is the Recordograph?

The recordograph is an accoustical device for making home recordings to be used with a record player or turn-table.

WHAT DO I GET?

You get the complete unit needed to make recordings at home. Accoustic recording head, special recording needle, playback needles, 6 two-sided records (enough for 12 recordings), spiral feeding attachment and complete easy to follow directions.

SING

PLAY

GREETINGS

RADIO PROGRAMS

BABY'S VOICE

PLAYS BACK AT ONCE

Record jokes, imitations, voices and instruments — and play for happy, happy memories. You can play new record at once! Give yourself, your family and friends a thrill! Records can be played back on ANY phonograph.

SING - PLAY - TALK

Have lots of fun! Record voices of seldom-seen but well-loved friends and dear ones. Make greeting records — Birthday, Anniversary Greetings for your loved ones.

EASY AS SPEAKING INTO A PHONE

Use your NEW HOME RECORD MAKER anytime and perform as comfortably as you'd talk on the telephone — needs no special "recording technique." *No experience necessary*

Records for 12 Recordings Included

Amazing, LOW Price only $8.49 COMPLETE

SEND NO MONEY!

You don't have to send a cent. Just fill in coupon and mail today to get your complete NEW HOME RECORD MAKER. Sent C.O.D. for only $8.49 plus postage and C.O.D. . . . or send check or money order for $3.49 and we pay postage.

Additional blank records $2.00 per dozen (24 sides)

RECORDOGRAPH CORP. OF AMERICA, Dept. TM–151
230 GRAND STREET, NEW YORK, N. Y.

Send entire RECORD MAKING OUTFIT, including 6 blank two-sided records.

☐ Send C.O.D. I will pay postman $8.49 plus postage.

☐ Send additional blank records at $2 per dozen.

Name _____

Address _____

City, Zone, State _____

☐ I enclose $8.49, send complete outfit postpaid.

WILL YOU WEAR THIS LOVELY

2-Way Jumper
ON APPROVAL

IT'S SMART! IT'S GAY!
It's Different!

It's a smart gal who takes to jumpers for a trim, Hollywood-born fashion that can be worn everywhere, any time. But it's a *smarter* gal who owns a chic jumper that can change — presto! — into still another glamorous outfit!

This Jaunty Jumper only $7.98

DOUBLE-DUTY!...DOUBLE-BEAUTY!

Completely *new* is this Jaunty Jumper, gorgeously tailored to flatter your figure in exquisite feminine lines. Completely *different* because you have *two jumpers in one:* wear it with the lovely contrasting color lapels opened in classic style . . . or button-closed into a demurely round neckline! Exclusively fashioned in crisp, fine-quality, all-season material that loves to "take it"! A slenderizing fitted waistband . . . freedom giving inverted pleat in the skirt add up to a knockout creation! Wear this sophisticated jumper and win compliments galore from men who admire your smart looks . . . women who envy your dual personality fashion! An original by Bonnie Gaye. Sizes 12 through 20 — and biggest of all surprises it's only $7.98 plus postage.

"BOW BLOUSE" — Tantalizing with its flattering high neck, perky bow, long full sleeves — it's a true complement to your jumper. In lustrous-rich rayon fabric. White only. Sizes 32 to 40. Only $3.98.

SEND NO MONEY — Check size and color choice and mail coupon today. On arrival, pay postman C.O.D. charges. Wear, compare. If a 10 day trial doesn't prove you've discovered the best buys ever, please return for full refund.

The illustration below shows how this sophisticated classic with open lapels can be changed into a demure feminine style with high round neck all through the simple but clever magic of buttons! Actually two jumpers in one!

10 DAYS' TRIAL
Yes, wear this Jaunty Jumper and "Bow Blouse" at MY RISK. If you are not completely satisfied in every way, return in 10 days and your full purchase price will be refunded. BONNIE GAYE.

Bonnie Gaye

MAIL COUPON TODAY!

BONNIE GAYE FASHIONS—Dept. 13-DD
168 N. Michigan Ave., Chicago 1, Ill.
Please send smart 2-WAY JUMPER. I'll pay postman $7.98 plus postage on arrival with the understanding I may return purchase for full refund if not satisfied in 10 days.

(Mark 1st and 2nd choice color selections)

Navy ☐   Brown ☐   Red ☐   Black ☐

(Circle Size)

12   14   16   18   20

Please send "BOW BLOUSE" at $3.98 plus postage (White Only)

(Circle Size)

32   34   36   38   40

NAME...

ADDRESS......................................

CITY............... ZONE...... STATE.........

Note: Order 2 jumpers for only $14.50 plus postage ☐

-1948-

87

EXAMINE IT FREE!

You, too, can learn how to make model planes that really fly . . . How to mystify your friends with magic . . . How to teach your dog tricks . . . How to do science stunts at home . . . How to have fun with electricity . . . How to toughen your muscles . . . How to build unusual radios . . . How to have fun with puzzles and hobbies . . . How to build a speedy soap-box racer and scores of other exciting things to do and make. Get this BOYS FUN BOOK. 192 pages, 470 pictures, bursting with sizzling ideas for your entertainment and amusement, all year 'round.

SEND NO MONEY. Just mail coupon. When book arrives, give postman only $1.49, plus delivery charge. If not delighted, money refunded within 7 days. If payment is sent with coupon, we pay delivery charges. Same guarantee applies. Mail coupon TODAY!

HOW TO FIX
ANY PART OF ANY CAR

USED BY U.S. ARMED FORCES

QUICKLY-- EASILY-- RIGHT!

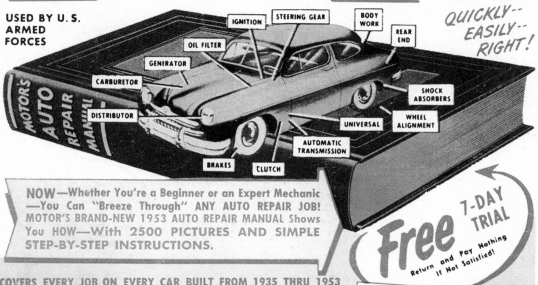

IGNITION STEERING GEAR BODY WORK REAR END OIL FILTER GENERATOR CARBURETOR DISTRIBUTOR SHOCK ABSORBERS UNIVERSAL WHEEL ALIGNMENT AUTOMATIC TRANSMISSION BRAKES CLUTCH

MOTORS AUTO REPAIR MANUAL

NOW—Whether You're a Beginner or an Expert Mechanic —You Can "Breeze Through" ANY AUTO REPAIR JOB! MOTOR'S BRAND-NEW 1953 AUTO REPAIR MANUAL Shows You HOW—With 2500 PICTURES AND SIMPLE STEP-BY-STEP INSTRUCTIONS.

Free 7-DAY TRIAL Return and Pay Nothing If Not Satisfied!

COVERS EVERY JOB ON EVERY CAR BUILT FROM 1935 THRU 1953

YES, it's easy as A-B-C to do any "fix-it" job on any car whether it's a simple carburetor adjustment or a complete overhaul. Just look up the job in the index of MOTOR'S New AUTO REPAIR MANUAL. Turn to pages covering job. Follow the clear, illustrated step-by-step instructions. Presto—the job is done!

No guesswork! MOTOR'S Manual takes nothing for granted. Tells you where to start. What tools to use. Then it leads you easily and quickly through the entire operation!

Over 2,500 Pictures! So Complete, So Simple, You CAN'T Go Wrong!

BRAND-NEW REVISED Edition covers everything you need to know to repair 907 car models. 850 giant pages, 2500 "This-Is-How" pictures. Over 200 "Quick-Check" charts—more than 37,000 essential repair specifications. Over 227,000 service and repair facts. Instructions and pictures are so clear you can't go wrong!

Even a green beginner mechanic can do a good job with this giant manual before him. And if you're a top-notch

mechanic, you'll find short-cuts that will amaze you. No wonder this guide is used by the U. S. Army and Navy! No wonder hundreds of thousands of men call it the "Auto Repair Man's Bible"!

Meat of Over 189 Official Shop Manuals

Engineers from every automobile plant in America worked out these time-saving procedures for their own motor car line. Now the editors of MOTOR have gathered together this wealth of "Know-How" from over 189 Official Shop Manuals, "boiled it down" into crystal-clear terms in one handy indexed book!

Same FREE Offer On MOTOR'S Truck and Tractor Manual
Covers EVERY job on EVERY popular make gasoline truck, tractor made from 1936 thru 1952. FREE 7-Day Trial. Check proper box in coupon.

Try Book FREE 7 Days

SEND NO MONEY! Just mail coupon! When the postman brings book, pay him nothing. First, make it show you what it's got! Unless you agree this is the greatest time-saver and work-saver you've ever seen — return book in 7 days and pay nothing. Mail coupon today! Address: *MOTOR Book Dept., Desk 28-A, 250 West 55th St., N. Y. 19, N. Y.*

Covers 907 Models—All These Makes

Buick	Henry J	Nash Rambler
Cadillac	Hudson	Oldsmobile
Chevrolet	Kaiser	Packard
Chrysler	Lafayette	Plymouth
Crosley	La Salle	Pontiac
De Soto	Lincoln	Studebaker
Dodge	Mercury	Terraplane
Ford	Nash	Willys
Frazer		

Many Letters of Praise from Users
"MOTOR'S Manual paid for itself on the first 2 jobs, and saved me valuable time by eliminating guesswork."
—W. SCHROP, Ohio.

He *Does Job in 30 Min.*—Fixed motor another mechanic had worked on half a day. With your Manual I did it in 30 minutes."
—C. AUBERRY, Tenn.

AMAZING NEW SCIENTIFIC METHOD

If you have blackheads, you know how embarrassing they are, how they clog your pores, mar your appearance and invite criticism. Now you can solve the problem of eliminating blackheads, forever, with this amazing new VACUTEX Invention. It extracts filthy blackheads in seconds, painlessly, without injuring or squeezing the skin. VACUTEX creates a gentle vacuum around blackhead! Cleans out hard-to-reach places in a jiffy. Germ laden fingers never touch the skin. Simply place the direction finder over blackhead, draw back extractor .. and it's out! Release extractor and blackhead is ejected. VACUTEX does it all! Don't risk infection with old-fashioned methods. Order TODAY!

10 DAY TRIAL OFFER

Don't wait until embarrassing criticism makes you act. Don't risk losing out on popularity and success because of ugly dirt-clogged pores. ACT NOW! Enjoy the thrill of having a clean skin, free of pore-clogging, embarrassing blackheads. Try Vacutex for 10 days. We guarantee it to do all we claim. If you are not completely satisfied your $1.00 will be immediately refunded.

ONLY THREE EASY STEPS

UGLY BLACKHEADS

USE VACUTEX

THEY'RE OUT!

RUSH COUPON • Send No MONEY

ACTUAL LENGTH 3½"

BALLCO PRODS. CO. Dept. 3601, 19 West 44th St., N.Y. 18, N.Y.

BALLCO PRODUCTS COMPANY, Dept. 3601
19 West 44th St., New York 18, N. Y.
☐ Ship C.O.D. I will pay postman $1.00 plus postage. My $1.00 will be refunded if I am not delighted.
☐ I prefer to enclose $1.00 now and save postage (Same guarantee as above)

NAME_____

ADDRESS_____

CITY_____ STATE_____